# Outlaws of Ravenhurst
# Study Guide

# Outlaws of Ravenhurst
# Study Guide

by

# Janet P. McKenzie

A RACE for Heaven Product

Biblio Resource Publications, Inc.
108½ South Moore Street
Bessemer, MI  49911
2009

ISBN 978-1-934185-24-7

Published by
Biblio Resource Publications, Inc.
108½ South Moore Street
Bessemer, MI 49911
inquiries@biblioresource.com
www.BiblioResource.com

With the exception of pronouns referring to God, rules of capitalization of religious and doctrinal terms follow the *Style Guide* of the United States Conference of Catholic Bishops, 2008.

A **R**ead **A**loud **C**urriculum **E**nrichment Product
www.RACEforHeaven.com

Printed in the United States of America

# Table of Contents

# Preface

L.M. Wallace wrote and illustrated *Outlaws of Raven-hurst* in 1923 for publication by Franciscan Herald Press. After undergoing considerable editing, Catholic Authors Press republished *Outlaws* in 1950, attributing authorship to the religious name of Sr. M. Imelda Wallace and adding illustrations created by Louis A. Schuster. Subsequently reprinted by several publishers, this exciting work of Catholic historical fiction has become a Catholic children's classic.

This study guide for the popular revised story of 1950 contains vocabulary words for each chapter in addition to aids designed to assist readers in assimilating the book's strong Catholic elements into their own daily lives. The questions and supplements focus on critical thinking, integration of Biblical teachings, and the study of the virtuous life to which Christ calls us as mature, confirmed Catholics. With its emphasis on the virtues (theological and moral plus the gifts and fruits of the Holy Spirit), the spiritual and the corporal works of mercy, and the Beatitudes, this study guide allows *Outlaws of Ravenhurst* to be utilized as catechetical tool for those preparing to receive the Sacrament of Confirmation. Use this exciting story as a living book to better understand the personality traits Christ wants us to develop and how we can live the "authentic Christian life" (*Compendium* of the *Catholic Church* ¶360) that the life and teachings of our Lord Jesus model for us.

i

# AIDS TO APPRECIATION
# FOR
# *OUTLAWS OF RAVENHURST*

# Introduction

In order to deepen your family's appreciation for *Outlaws of Ravenhurst* and to utilize this work of Catholic historical fiction as a catechetical tool, several areas of study are provided for each chapter. Definitions of more difficult or possibly unfamiliar words are given in addition to brief notations for historical names, events, and some geographical locations. The discussion questions provided for each chapter are intended to increase critical thinking skills. Scripture references are presented in the hope of connecting God's Word with daily living and to better familiarize families with God's great gift of Sacred Scripture.

Additionally, lessons on Christian living and the virtues have been created, especially for those preparing to receive the Sacrament of Confirmation. One virtue is studied with each chapter. The virtues include the theological virtues (faith, hope, and love), the four moral virtues (justice, prudence, temperance, and fortitude), the seven gifts of the Holy Spirit (wisdom, understanding, counsel, fortitude, knowledge, piety, and fear of the Lord), and most of the twelve fruits of the Holy Spirit. Matching exercises (with corresponding answer keys) on the corporal and spiritual works of mercy and the Beatitudes are also included.

## Instructions for use

After each day's reading is complete, review the vocabulary words as needed and discuss the questions provided for each chapter. Use the Scripture connections as desired. Consider memorizing some of the referenced Scripture passages.

To utilize the virtue study, briefly study and discuss the definition of each chapter's virtue. Then re-read the passage given in which a character from the story demonstrates this virtue. Complete the virtue study by conducting a short discussion on the given virtue in action. One possible format for this discussion is provided, but be willing to vary the conversation from chapter to chapter. Utilize the matching exercises on the works of mercy and the Beatitudes upon completion of the book.

# Chapter 1 – The Gray-Cloaked Stranger

## Vocabulary
1. *spars*: long poles to which sails are fastened; masts
2. *dory*: flat-bottomed boat
3. *smother*: a confused multitude of things

## Discussion Questions
1. There is an air of mystery and secrecy in this first chapter. Speculate on what is happening. What do you think the plan of the "gray-cloaked stranger" is?
2. Consider who or what the man is who had "the appearance of a missionary passing from one Mass station to another."

## Scripture References
1. Read the story of another child who traveled under the cover of darkness due to danger in Matthew 2:13-15.
2. Read the story of Moses, another child who was purposely placed, in Exodus 2:1-10.

## Virtue – Kindness (Benignity): The expression of sympathy and concern for those in trouble or need; can be shown in words, deeds, or acts of forgiveness for injuries sustained; one of the fruits of the Holy Spirit

## Virtue Passage
Although the gray-clocked stranger was firm in his mission, he conducted himself with great kindness: Read the following passage from Chapter 1:

> Keen and marrow-searching, the morning wind rose along the shore of Maryland. Dense fog became a fine, drizzling rain turning to sleet. Breasting it

along lonely ways among the sand dunes, hurried a lean, bent man carrying a bundle under his cloak—a long, muddied, thread-bare garment as gray as rain-soaked ashes.

The bundle was hard to manage. It seemed to move of its own accord. Once in a while, a sound came out of it, a wailing cry, "Dunkie Teewee! Take Dordie out."

"Sh!" the man would whisper. His tone was a stern command, but his eyes glowed with great love. The bundle would sniffle a moment or two, then grow quiet.

After hours of tramping, the man found a nook where the forest met the last sand dunes. Here, crouched between a low bank and a tree, with his own body shielding the bundle from the sleet, the man opened his cloak and loosened the sailcloth and the plaid shawl within. A fat fist slipped out of the opening, then a tousle of brown curls, a gurgling laugh, and a piping voice, "Dood Dunkie Tee-wee! Take it all off!"

"Hush!" came the man's low command in a tone that would have been menacing except that it was so deeply kind. "Drink." He drew a flask from his cloak.

The child drank, but all the while he stared over the bottle's rim at the man—a wise, wide, baby stare. His eyes were blue and deep as the sea, with a flash in their depths that in the turning of an instant might be fun or fury; just now the eyes shone with a puzzled and half-angry trust.

Even in this short time the little fist which guided the flask was growing blue though it gripped with deft strength—a swordsman's right hand still in the making. The stranger hastened to enclose the baby in his warm coverings. He wound the cloak about himself and his bundle, left the shelter, and hurried on through the stinging sleet.

## Virtue Discussion

1. Discuss this passage. Can you recall any incidents from the lives of the saints that demonstrate kindness?
2. Consider a time in your life when you or someone you know practiced this virtue. What was the effect of this action? Discuss at least two specific things you can do differently in your daily life to improve your practice of the virtue of kindness. Do them!

# Chapter 2 – Brown-Head Goes Fishing

## Vocabulary
1. *flintlock gun*: a type of gun that has a flint in the hammer to strike a metal plate, causing a spark to ignite the gunpowder
2. *muzzle-loader*: a gun that is loaded through the open end of the barrel
3. *alders*: small, rapidly growing trees; members of the birch family

## Discussion Questions
1. Relating this chapter to the first chapter, speculate on how these "twins" can look so differently.
2. "There was nothing in his tone to show which boy was his son." Explain this statement.

## Scripture References
1. Read about the birth of the twins Esau—a red-head—and Jacob in Genesis 25:19-27.
2. Like George, in his youth King David killed a bear. Read 1 Samuel 17:32-37. Read and discuss Proverb 17:12.

**Virtue – Goodness:** the exercise of the will to keep the divine commands and the precepts of nature; those actions consistent with God's nature, and suitable and befitting a Child of God; one of the fruits of the Holy Spirit

## Virtue Passage
Read about George's goodness to his twin brother Joel in the following passage from Chapter 2:

Joel gave a sharp cry. George turned. "What's the matter with you? Quick! She's swimming!"

"I stepped on my fishhook!"

"Pull it out! She's comin'!"

"Can't! It's all the way in!"

"Here! Let me get hold of it!"

"Ow! Don't!"

"You got to stand it! She's halfway over! There, it's out! Come on now!"

"Oh! I can't step! Ow!"

"You've turned your ankle! Lean on me! Hop! She's almost here! Hop! I'll help you!"

"Go on, George, save yourself!"

"Do you think I'd leave you? Here, try to climb this tree."

"Too little! She can climb. Go on! You can run. Go on, George, quick!"

"Quit cryin'! Climb! I'll boost you!"

At last, Joel was astride a crotch in the tree. George looked at his white face, jerked off both their belts, buckled them together, slipped one end of the strap around Joel's waist, twisted the rest around the limb a couple of times, and fastened it securely.

## Virtue Discussion

1. Discuss this passage. Can you recall any incidents from the lives of the saints that demonstrate this virtue?

2. Consider a time in your life when you or someone you know practiced this virtue. What was the effect of this action? Discuss at least two specific things you can do differently in your daily life to improve your practice of the virtue of goodness. Do them!

# Chapter 3 – Uncle Roger

## Vocabulary
1. *Cecil Calvert*: Second Lord Baltimore; obtained a charter from England's King Charles I for the colony of Maryland, established as a Catholic refuge; Lord Proprietor of Maryland from 1632-1675
2. *squire*: judge
3. *the beads*: rosary
4. *gauntlet*: long glove, usually of leather to protect the hand; may be thrown down in combat to challenge an opponent
5. *scion*: descendant or heir of an influential family
6. *Sir Archibald Bell-the-Cat*: Archibald Douglas, fifth Earl of Angus (1449-1513); earned the name "Bell the Cat" in his battle with Robert Cochrane in 1482 at Lauder, Scotland
7. *pipkin*: a small cooking pot

## Discussion Questions
1. "No man can lead you into sin if you don't follow him." What do you think this means? How can you apply this quotation to your own life?
2. What characteristic did Roger recognize in Gordon's eyes that caused him concern?

## Scripture References
1. George obeyed Mary's quiet voice when she asked him to obey his uncle. Read and discuss Colossians 3:20.
2. Read Proverb 16:8. How can you apply this lesson to what you know about the Abells and Roger Gordon?

**Virtue – Piety:** Honor or reverence given to someone in any way responsible for our existence or well-being such as God as our Creator and constant Provider, our parents, or our country; leads to devotion to God; one of the seven gifts of the Holy Spirit

## Virtue Passage

Although upset and confused, George demonstrates the virtue of piety by unwaveringly obeying his mother—and defending her:

> The twins struggled down from the soldier's saddle and ran to their mother. But, as Walter came forward with the horse, George drew his hand from his uncle's grasp. "I want to say good-by, please," he said.
>
> "Walter, give the young gentleman your hand to mount. We have wasted too much time as it is."
>
> "I'm going to stay till I say good-by," flashed the boy, "and I won't go before."
>
> "Do as you are bid, George." It was Mary's quiet voice.
>
> "Yes, Mother," and the boy mounted.
>
> The horsemen trotted back across the field and down the road, but the boy's face was turned toward the wood. The little group among the trees dropped out of sight. The cabin came and went. As the last bit of smoke was hidden by the trees, the brave lips began to tremble, and the tears came, burning-hot and choking. Sir Roger gave a signal. The troop swung forward, leaving him and his nephew alone.
>
> "Is this the gratitude you show to the uncle who has come overseas in search of you?"
>
> "I wanted to say good-by. You wouldn't let me even kiss Mother or tell Joel—"
>
> "Kiss? Such dirty—"
>
> "They are not dirty—only from hard work since sunup. They are my folk. Joel, he's my twin. I mean,

I always thought he was—"

"Your folk!" cried the gentleman with a laugh. "But you do not know, as yet, who or what you are. You are Charles Gordon, Lord Rock Raven, the son of James Gordon, Lord of Rock Raven, third Earl of Ravenhurst. Your mother is Lady Margaret of Douglas, daughter of Sir Wilfrid Douglas of the line of old Sir Archibald Bell-the-Cat. There are few in Scotland that can boast such blood as yours. And you are weeping for your folk! The folk of the heir of Ravenhurst!" He laughed again. "John Abell, lord of a log cabin and a pigsty, in size an ox, in brain a pipkin. . . his most noble dame with a face as wrinkled and brown as the apple she baked last Candlemas. . .a dozen—nay, was it fourteen—red-headed brats. . .and these are the folk of the scion of Ravenhurst!"

A light leaped far down in those deep-blue Douglas eyes, a flame that burned up boyish tears, leaving a white-hot anger that Roger both knew and feared.

Gordon answered: "Sir, poor or not, the Abells are my folk."

## Virtue Discussion

1. Discuss this passage. Can you recall any incidents from the lives of the saints that demonstrate this virtue?

2. Consider a time in your life when you or someone you know practiced this virtue. What was the effect of this action? Discuss at least two specific things you can do differently in your daily life to improve your practice of the virtue of piety. Do them!

# Chapter 4 – When Men Play Marbles

## Vocabulary

1. *earl*: title awarded by a king to a chieftain who ruled a given territory in the stead of the king; wife's title would be "Lady"
2. *frith*: a long, narrow inlet or arm of the sea where a river current meets the tide; also firth
3. *marauders*: those who roam about, raiding and plundering
4. *claymore*: a large, double-edged sword
5. *bracken*: area overgrown with thickets of large, coarsely-leafed ferns
6. *warden*: official in charge of a specific territory
7. *James Stuart*: King James V (1512-1542) ruled Scotland from the age of 17 months until his death following a mental collapse
8. *galley*: a large, open boat propelled by oars
9. *Lord of Arran*: possibly James Hamilton (1516-1575), Third Lord of Arran
10. *Argyll*: possibly Gillespie Roy Archibald Campbell (1507-1558), the fourth Earl of Argyll
11. *Russell*: probably John Russell (1485-1555), the First Baron Russell and later Earl of Bedford
12. *morasses*: areas of low-lying, soggy ground; marshes or swamps
13. *Bluff Hall of England*: common nickname for King Henry VIII, who reigned England from 1509 to 1547

## Discussion Questions

1. What might change in your family if "the word 'I cannot' is not said" in your house?

2. Just as Lang-Sword gained royal favor by jumping into the sea to deliver a message, what might we do to gain good favor with our Lord, Jesus Christ?

## Scripture References
1. Read what our Lord says about "cannot" in Luke 14:27.
2. Read and discuss what Proverbs suggest regarding gaining favor with the king or the Lord: 8:32-36, 14:35, 16:12-15, and 19:12.

**Virtue – Justice:** The cardinal (moral) virtue that consists of the constant and firm will to give to God and to neighbor their due; giving to others what by right belongs to them

## Virtue Passage
In the following passage, notice how Gordon does not hesitate to profess Fire-the-Braes' behavior as unjust.

> Now, Fire-the-Braes was a bold and bloody man. He carried a long two-handed claymore the like of which no other man ever bore. From his wild and lonely tower on Rock Raven he sallied out for daring raids, driving home cattle, plundering, burning villages and harvest fields. It was for this he was dubbed Fire-the-Braes, a name of terror from the Isles to the English border—"
>
> "An out-and-out villain and robber!" cried the boy.

## Virtue Discussion
1. Discuss this passage. Can you recall any incidents from the lives of the saints that demonstrate the virtue of justice?

2. Consider a time in your life when you or someone you know practiced this virtue. What was the effect of this action? Discuss at least two specific things you can do differently in your daily life to improve your practice of justice. Do them!

# Chapter 5 – Castle Ravenhurst

## Vocabulary

1. *scabbard*: a sheath or covering for a sword or dagger
2. *lee*: that side opposite or away from the wind
3. *Solway Moss*: battle fought in November 1542 between King James V and King Henry VIII near the River Esk
4. *regent*: a person who governs instead of the rightful sovereign in times of minority, absence, or disability
5. *elfin*: having a magical charm or quality; otherworldly
6. *lowlanders*: those who reside in the Scottish Lowlands; Scotland is divided into roughly three geographical regions: the Highlands, the Central Plain and the Southern Lowlands; the Lowlands contains the latter two regions or roughly half the country
7. *new faith*: faith of the National Scottish Church (The Kirk) established after the Scottish Reformation of 1560 when it broke from the Roman Catholic Church
8. *bawbees*: Scottish coins of small value, such as a halfpenny
9. *moat*: a deep, wide trench surrounding a fortified place and filled with water
10. *tapestry*: a heavy, woven cloth with picture designs used for hanging or upholstery
11. *carpet-knight*: one not knighted on the field of battle but dubbed by Court as a favor; a knight who spends his time in luxury and idleness
12. *lairds*: Scottish lords or owners of landed estates

## Discussion Questions

1. Discuss Godfrey's idea of "ridding" Gordon of the Catholic faith. How can we nourish our faith?
2. Why did Roger inform Lady Gordon of the "laws concerning the imparting of knowledge on certain dangerous subjects to youth of our land?" Why would the Catholic faith be considered a dangerous subject? Who or what might it endanger?

## Scripture References

1. Read and discuss the following Scripture passages: Wisdom 16:20, Sirach 15:1-7, and Ephesians 6:16.
2. Regarding Lady Gordon's portrayal as "a mother eagle guarding her young," read Exodus 19:3-6 and Psalm 91:1-4.

**Virtue – Modesty:** Grounded in humility, that fruit of the Holy Spirit that moderates our behavior toward others and inclines us to recognize our own worth in true light; purity in words, actions, and dress; helps us to avoid what is offensive to others as well as those things that are unnecessary

## Virtue Passage

Gordon has not let his rank go to his head. Read the following passage, which illustrates Gordon's modesty:

> From the seaward tower came a puff of white smoke and then a roar. Sir Roger rose in the carriage, lifting his plumed hat. Over the water the sound of a great bell rolled. The rocks caught the echo, and many an elfin note made answer from crag and cliff and forest far up, even to the summit of old Ben Ender.
>
> "What is all this noise about?" whispered the lad. "Tell me, Godfrey, or I shall make a blunder."

"Will you never learn that you are the scion of the House of Gordon? The cannon and the bells of old Ravenhurst are welcoming you, my Lord."

## Virtue Discussion

1. Discuss this passage. Can you recall any incidents from the lives of the saints that further demonstrate the virtue of modesty?
2. Consider a time in your life when you or someone you know practiced this virtue. What was the effect of this action? Discuss at least two specific things you can do differently in your daily life to improve your practice of modesty. Do them!

# Chapter 6 – By the Old Fireplace

## Vocabulary

1. *'wee bit bairnie'*: In Scottish, a bairn is a child or a baby.
2. *yeomen*: officers or manservants in a noble or royal household
3. *whetstone*: a hard, smooth stone used to sharpen knives and tools
4. *medal (mettle)*: basic character; spirit; courage
5. *wampum*: beads made of small shells and strung on thread; used as money by Native Americans
6. *dragoons*: soldiers trained to fight on foot but who often traveled by horseback; can be classified as "light" or "heavy" dragoons
7. *last rites*: the Sacraments of Penance and Reconciliation, Anointing of the Sick (formerly called Extreme Unction), and Viaticum (Holy Eucharist) given to a person before death
8. *frigate*: a fast, medium-sized warship
9. *fastnesses*: remote, secret places; strongholds
10. *glens*: narrow, secluded valleys
11. *the Bruce*: Robert the Bruce, King of Scotland from 1306-1329

## Discussion Questions

1. "The Earl of Ravenhurst must always stand for God and our Blessed Lady, let the cost be what it may." What are some costs of practicing the Catholic faith and being devoted to our Blessed Mother today?
2. Discuss the following quotation: ". . .saints do not reason as worldly people do."
3. Against what and whom did Margaret warn her son?

21

## Scripture References

1. Regarding the "great white throne," read Revelation 20:11-12.
2. In reference to "Holy! Holy! Holy! Lord God of Hosts!" see Revelation 4:1-11 and Isaiah 6:1-4.
3. Gordon's mother refers to his soul as a pearl. In many cultures, a pearl is a symbol of great worth. Read the parable where Jesus compares the Kingdom of Heaven to a pearl of great price: Matthew 13:45-46.

**Virtue – Faithfulness:** The fruit of the Holy Spirit that allows us to constantly submit our will and intellect to God and to the truth the Catholic Church proclaims

## Virtue Passage

Read the following passage from Chapter 6 that shows both Gordon's and his mother's faithfulness:

Oh, why did everyone hate the Faith he had been taught to love? His hand gripped the arm of the chair till the knuckles stood out hard and white; yet, he looked straight into those stern eyes and answered:

"The Abells are Catholics, and I am a Catholic, too."

His mother was not looking at him now. Her eyes were fixed on the old fireplace with a look of deepest joy. "Holy Mother of God," she was saying, "I thank thee that thou hast kept thy trust."

"Mother, if you are a Catholic, what made you look at me like that?"

"I wished to learn of what metal you are formed, my son. There is one weakling in the House of Gordon. Had you shown a spirit like Sir Roger's, had your will bent because you feared me, I would have disowned you, my son, though it broke my heart.

"The Earl of Ravenhurst must always stand for God and our blessed Lady, let the cost be what it may."

## Virtue Discussion

1. Discuss this passage. Can you recall any incidents from the lives of the saints that demonstrate faithfulness?

2. Consider a time in your life when you or someone you know practiced this virtue. What was the effect of this action? Discuss at least two specific things you can do differently in your daily life to improve your practice of the virtue of faithfulness. Do them!

# Chapter 7 – My Friend Godfrey

## Vocabulary

1. ***Candlemas***: the ceremony of the blessing and distribution of candles to celebrate Simeon's prophecy of Christ as a light to the Gentiles (Luke 2:32); celebrated February 2; now known as the Feast of the Purification

2. ***this day fortnight***: a fortnight is a period of fourteen consecutive days. "This day fortnight" would be two weeks from today.

3. ***countenance***: appearance, especially the expression of the face

4. ***inkhorn***: a small, round container made of horn or a similar material that holds ink for writing

5. ***scribe***: a writer or journalist; a learned person

6. ***sarcasm***: a mocking, often ironic, remark intended to hurt

7. ***soldiery***: military personnel; the profession of soldiering; soldiers as a group

8. ***battlement***: a narrow wall built along the edge or top of a castle wall for protection; has open spaces for shooting

9. ***Orkneys to Lands End***: Lands End and the Orkney Islands are situated in the far south and far north ends of the island of Britain, respectively

10. ***bonny***: pleasing to the eye; attractive; fine

11. ***prig***: a snob; someone who is annoying and arrogant

12. ***plumes***: large, showy feathers

13. ***curlew***: a long-legged, brown shorebird

14. ***sward***: grass-covered soil; lawn

15. ***forsooth***: in truth; no doubt

16. ***House of Lords***: the upper house of Parliament or the legislature in Great Britain (The lower house is

called the "House of Commons."); similar to the House of Congress in the United States

17. *maid of honor*: a female attendant to the Queen; sometimes a paid position, sometimes unpaid

18. *wainscoting*: wooden paneling used to line the walls of a room

## Discussion Questions

1. How can you explain the discrepancies between Godfrey and Roger's description of Gordon's mother with Gordon's memory of that first night at Ravenhurst?

2. Godfrey accuses Gordon of being a dreamer with a dream-mother and a dream-church. What are the advantages and drawbacks of seeing things in a positive light—of being a dreamer?

## Scripture References

1. In reference to Gordon's statement that his mother's hair was snow-white, read Proverb 16:31.

2. Godfrey compares the Church to a tree. St. Paul compares the Church to a living building in Ephesians 2:19-22, and portrays it as the Body of Christ in 1 Corinthians 12:12-26 and Ephesians 1:22-23. To what would you compare the Church? (Remember that the Church is not just a building. The people of faith—the family of God—are the living stones of the Church.)

**Virtue – Understanding:** A gift of the Holy Spirit that provides insight into the mysteries of faith and how to live them

## Virtue Passage

Read Gordon's explanation of the Church and truth that shows the gift of understanding that he has received from the Holy Spirit:

> "Oh, no, Godfrey! Are the oaks dead because the leaves have fallen? Neither is the Church of God dead!"
>
> "Now, bravo! There is eloquence as well as wit in that. Your brain will be as keen in argument as was Lang-Sword's steel in battle. Let your training be what it should, and, mark my words, the day will come when the House of Lords, aye, even the king himself, will hang breathless upon your words."
>
> "Oh, it is not that I know how to argue, but you have the wrong side, Godfrey. The side that is not true always has a hole in it."

## Virtue Discussion

1. Discuss this passage. Can you recall any incidents from the lives of the saints that demonstrate this virtue?
2. Consider a time in your life when you or someone you know practiced this virtue. What was the effect of this action? Discuss at least two specific things you can do differently in your daily life to improve your practice of the virtue of understanding. Do them!

# Chapter 8 – The Ruin in the Wood

## Vocabulary

1. *parchment*: a superior quality paper that resembles sheepskin
2. *conquest*: someone whose affections have been won
3. *altar rail*: a horizontal bar that separates the sanctuary from the body of the church; when Holy Communion is received by the faithful on their knees, may be called the communion rail as the faithful line up kneeling in front of this rail and take turns receiving our Lord's Body and Blood
4. *Cross of Malta*: an eight-pointed star symbolic of the military order of the Knights of Malta
5. *cloister*: a covered walk that runs along the walls of monastery or convent buildings
6. *minster*: church of a monastery or convent
7. *stalls*: the fixed seats of the choir, wholly or partially enclosed on the back and sides, where the Divine Office is chanted
8. *moldering*: disintegrating; becoming rotten
9. *gray cloak*: the habit of a member of the First Order of the Franciscans or the Gray Friars; established by St. Francis of Assisi in 1209
10. *dungeons*: dark, underground cells of a castle; used as a prison
11. *friar*: a monk or brother who works outside a monastery
12. *mite*: a small amount
13. *dross*: worthless material; scum

## Discussion Questions

1. "He thought of the promises, boyish promises, earnest, loving, whispered to the Lord Jesus." Think of the promises you have made to Jesus, especially after

receiving Him in Holy Communion. What can you do to help yourself follow through on these promises?

2. Stephen's heart was full of joy as he heard Gordon ask to receive the sacraments. Why did Stephen ask Gordon if he was now ready to suffer for God?

## Scripture References

1. Gordon escapes the fate of Absolom, the son of King David. Read about this incident in 2 Samuel 18:9.
2. Stephen calls Godfrey "a devil with the oil of flattery upon his lips." Read about flattery in Sirach 41:14-16.

**Virtue – Faith:** The theological virtue by which we believe in God and all that He has said and revealed to us

## Virtue Passage

Read how Gordon's faith is renewed as he recalls saying the rosary and receiving his First Holy Communion:

> Gordon slipped the beads through his fingers. They brought memories: the old cabin, Mother kneeling by the cradle rocking it with her foot, Father leading the prayers, and all the little Abells answering, "Holy Mary Mother of God, pray for us sinners." He saw Daddy reaching one hairy hand to give little Which a cuff for tickling Tother's feet, but never pausing in the prayer. Then he remembered the old log church. Father Cornwall's solemn voice, but still the same sweet prayer that the angel said: "Hail Mary, full of grace." And the great day—it was only a year ago— when they made their First Communion, he and Joel. He thought of the joy of that moment when, kneeling at the altar rail, he saw the priest raise the Host above the chalice and the long-awaited moment had come. He thought of the promises, boyish promises, earnest, loving, whispered to the Lord Jesus.

Read too in the following passage how his faith impels him to receive the sacraments:

> "Uncle Stephen, Mother said you are a priest."
>
> "Well, I am, child."
>
> "Then couldn't I . . . couldn't I . . . go to confession to you here? And I am fasting. Perhaps . . . that is . . . is there any way for me to receive Holy Communion? Maybe then I wouldn't be so. . . ."
>
> Friar Stephen took the tear-stained face in his hands.
>
> "I have frightened you overmuch, my son. You have been sorely tempted, but I do not think that you have sinned grievously. If Sir Roger were to hear that you had received the sacraments, he would be very angry."
>
> "He often gets angry. I shall not mind that."
>
> "This will be a very different sort of anger. He is cruel, as all cowards are. There will be no one who will dare to defend you." Stephen spoke slowly, as if weighing his words; yet he knew what the answer would be.
>
> "My father suffered, and Mother is suffering now."
>
> There was joy in the soul of Stephen Douglas. Many were the prayers he had said, many the penances offered that this day might come.
>
> "So you are ready, Gordon, ready to take your first step on the path of those who suffer for God." Then, taking a kerchief from his cloak pocket, the friar began to bind it over the boy's eyes.
>
> "Why are you covering my eyes?" cried the startled lad.
>
> "It is not wise for you to know where the good Lord is hiding."

"Do you think I would tell?" cried Gordon, cut to the heart.

"No, no, child! You would not tell. I did not mean that, but Godfrey will ask sharp questions and judge by your face when he finds the truth. Bertrand's son is cunning, but he cannot learn from you what you do not know. So, you will go with the bandages over your eyes. There is a long walk before you. Say your prayers as you go."

A long walk it was indeed, with many turns and twists. At last Friar Stephen spoke.

"Be careful now! We are to go down steps."

Down, down, down they went, and then on again. It was damp and cold. Gordon knew it was a cellar but never thought the prudent friar had led him about in the wood only to take him into the same ruin from which he had brought him. At last, Stephen turned a key in a lock, opened a door, and removed the bandages. They were in a place that Gordon could scarcely see. No little trembling light burned through the darkness. The enemies were too many. Only the holy stillness spoke of the Guest Divine, and Gordon knelt to adore.

## Virtue Discussion

1. Discuss this passage. Can you recall any incidents from the lives of the saints that illustrate this virtue?
2. Consider a time in your life when you or someone you know practiced this virtue. What was the effect of this action? Discuss at least two specific things you can do differently in your daily life to improve your practice of the virtue of faith. Do them!

# Chapter 9 – The Mercy of a Coward

## Vocabulary
1. *skylark*: playful; frolicking; boisterous
2. *Mary, Queen of Scots*: daughter of King James V; crowned Queen before she was a week old in 1542; reigned (despite imprisonment) as Queen of Scotland until her execution for alleged conspiracy to kill Queen Elizabeth of England in 1587
3. *adversary*: an opponent; an enemy
4. *skulking*: moving about secretly; lurking; hiding or practicing evasion
5. *cutthroat*: an unprincipled, dangerous person; a murderer
6. *sallow*: an unnatural or sickly pale complexion
7. *scaffold*: a platform used for the execution of prisoners by hanging or beheading
8. *bloodhounds*: dogs trained to track by scent; any type of relentless pursuers
9. *imprudence*: the quality of being offensively bold and rude

## Discussion Questions
1. "But sacraments have a strong effect on those who have as strong a faith in them as Gordon has." Do you think that the amount of grace we receive from the sacraments depends on the amount of faith we have?
2. Why do you think that Godfrey told Gordon, "Friar Douglas often binds the eyes of children whom he thinks too young to trust?" What does this statement tell us about Godfrey's character?
3. What does "The Mercy of a Coward" mean?

## Scripture References

1. "Wine, nothing but wine." See Mark 14:22-25 and 1 Corinthians 11:23-26.
2. True to the prophecy of Stephen, Gordon begins to suffer for his faith when he is whipped by Uncle Roger. Read about St. Paul's sufferings in 2 Corinthians 11:24-27.

**Virtue – Self-control (Continence):** The act, power, or habit of having one's desires under the control of the will; a fruit of the Holy Spirit

## Virtue Passage

Read about Roger's loss of self-control as contrasted with Gordon's perseverance:

Sir Roger struck quick, sharp blows while he spoke. The lash hissed through the air and writhed around the slim body again and again. The child staggered this way and that from the force of the blows. Once or twice, when the burning whip struck the rising welts, there came a sharp cry. That was all. He did not say one word.

Sir Roger's arm was growing tired, but the square jaw was still set, and the blue eyes looked straight into his. He began to realize that the boy's will was stronger than his own. "Weakling of the House of Gordon!" That taunt had been thrown at him since childhood, and now, here was a boy with a will stronger than his own. Pride stung him. The whip fell again and again, but Gordon saw that the coward was weakening. The light of victory shone in the blazing Douglas eyes. There was new courage in every line of that little body still staggering under the weight of the blows.

The look in Gordon's eyes stung Sir Roger's pride anew. Yield? Godfrey had seen everything. Yield? Even the groom would sneer. He tried to strike with the same force as before, but his arm was weary, aching. The whip dropped. He had not the power to give what the lad had the courage to take.

## Virtue Discussion

1. Discuss this passage. Can you recall any incidents from the lives of the saints that demonstrate self-control?

2. Consider a time in your life when you or someone you know practiced this virtue. What was the effect of this action? Discuss at least two specific things you can do differently in your daily life to improve your self-control. Do them!

# Chapter 10 — Secret of the Fireplace

## Vocabulary
1. **gallivanting**: traveling or roaming about in search of pleasure
2. **gay**: given to social pleasures
3. **frolic**: scene of fun and merriment
4. **hilt**: the handle of a weapon or tool
5. **muzzle**: the forward part of an animal's face including mouth, nose, and jaws; the snout
6. **dogged**: stubbornly persistent; unyielding

## Discussion Questions
1. Betsy tells Gordon that shortly after Lady Margaret disappeared, Godfrey, who feeds the prisoners, "began to get two extra portions from the cook." For whom do you think the two extra portions were?
2. Name several ways that Lady Margaret prepared her son in the event of religious persecution and trial.

## Scripture References
1. Like Gordon, the prophet Jeremiah was beaten and imprisoned. Read Jeremiah 37: 15-16.
2. Read and discuss Romans 8:35-37, 2 Timothy 3:12-15, and 1 Peter 2:19-23 on trials and persecution.

**Virtue — Patience:** A fruit of the Holy Spirit that enables us to endure the evils caused by another without sadness or resentment in conformity with the will of God; a form of fortitude

## Virtue Passage
Re-read the following three paragraphs in which we see how Gordon's sorrow and self-pity are transformed into patient tolerance for his sufferings:

Shaken and weary, the lad stumbled to the armchair and flung himself into it, but the chair awakened memories of his mother. Sorrow welled up in him, and the pain of his wounds rose with the lull in excitement. A moan burst from his lips, but it was choked on the instant.

"No!" he muttered, "Uncle Roger shall never hear a whine from me. He shall never see the mark of a tear. He can do without that much fun!" Then slowly the thought dawned on his mind, "And . . . and . . . in a way . . .I did deserve what I got. No boy was ever so mean to his own mother."

Gordon slid down on his knees and knelt a long time with his head bowed on the old chair.

## Virtue Discussion

1. Discuss this passage. Can you recall any incidents from the lives of the saints that demonstrate patience?

2. Consider a time in your life when you or someone you know practiced this virtue. What was the effect of this action? Discuss at least two specific things you can do differently in your daily life to improve your practice of the virtue of patience. Do them!

# Chapter 11 – Return of Lang-Sword

## Vocabulary
1. *waggish*: humorous
2. *rampart*: an embankment for protection or defense
3. *garrison*: an established military post where troops reside; may also refer to the troops themselves
4. *retinue*: a group of servants or assistants who accompany an important person
5. *mail*: flexible armor made of small overlapping metal rings
6. *chivalry*: the ethical code, customs, and principles of knighthood
7. *largess*: gifts and/or money
8. *turrets*: small towers extending above the buildings
9. *benediction*: a divine blessing or protection
10. **Te Deum**: ancient hymn of praise and thanksgiving to God; name derives from the first words of the hymn, *"Te Deum Laudamus"* or "We praise you, O God"; originates from around the fourth century
11. *relic*: an object connected with a saint; something they used, part of their body, or something they had touched
12. *friary*: a community of friars, or the residence in which they live
13. *Tertiary*: member of the Third Order Secular that includes members of either sex who live in the world and do not wear a religious habit, but follow a religious rule of life
14. *Flodden Field*: site of a battle fought between the forces of King James IV of Scotland and King Henry VIII of England on September 9, 1513 in Northumberland; the Scots were defeated with ten thousand Scottish men killed including King James IV

15. *spoils*: goods or property taken by violence
16. *friar warden*: the superior of a religious house; now called "Guardian"
17. *lazaretto*: a hospital where those with infectious diseases are treated
18. **Ave**: *Ave Maria* is Latin for Hail Mary
19. *pibroch*: military music played by highland bagpipes; often a traditional dirge (mournful funeral hymn)
20. *ensigns*: military banners, standards and/or flags
21. *esquire*: attendant and shield bearer to a knight
22. *inmates*: persons living with others in the same building
23. *baskined feet*: feet covered with thick-soled, laced boots that go partially up the legs; also feet that drag due to tragedy
24. *biercloth*: a cloth that covers a corpse or coffin
25. *armorer*: person skilled in making arms and weapons; someone who is in charge of the upkeep of small arms
26. *bills*: weapons with hooked blades mounted on short staffs
27. *obeisance*: bowing or bending of the knee as a gesture of homage or submission

## Discussion Questions

1. In what ways do you think the Church in Scotland served as a "great source of unity?"
2. As she received our Lord in Holy Communion, what sacrifice did Lady Gordon offer to our Lord? What sacrifice can you offer to our Lord when you receive Him in the most Blessed Sacrament?
3. How can you apply Lady Gordon's cry, "No cause is lost while true hearts live!" to your daily life?

## Scripture References
1. "Ever since the Holy Three made blessed the home in Nazareth. . . ." Read Matthew 2:19-23 and Luke 2:39-40.
2. Read the following Scripture passages on unity: 1 Corinthians 1:10-11, 2 Corinthians 13:11, Galatians 3:28, and Ephesians 4:3.

**Virtue – Peace:** A calm that accompanies the agreement of human wills upon which every well-ordered society rests; a fruit of the Holy Spirit; tranquility of order

## Virtue Passage
Read the description of the disorder in Scotland in the following passage. Reflect on the role of Lang-Sword and King James V in restoring peace to this war-torn land:

*Lang-Sword had come into power in time to face the dangers that Fire-the-Braes had feared. The centuries of family feuds had left Scot so bitter against Scot that it was impossible to present a truly united front against any enemy.*

*In past generations, at least in moments of national peril, family quarrels would be forgotten. In the bloody circle of Flodden Field around the royal standard of James IV they stood: Border spears and Perthshire men, Fife and Gordon, Merse and Argyll— feuds forgotten and hearts aflame for Scotland while rank by rank the red English bills cut them down. Grim death clutched them man by man, but none faltered and none fled. Yeomen, spearmen, archer, knight, and earl twisted in one mass of dying men; till, with a crash which shakes the soul of Scotland yet, the King charged—and charging fell, his lifeblood flowing on the silken banner of our land, down trodden on Flodden Field.*

*So were the Scots from before the days of Fire-the-Braes till James IV—ruining Scotland by their endless petty feuds yet loving Scotland to the death, while among them, stirring up strife at all times, went traitors paid with foreign gold.*

*Beside this strong spirit of national loyalty, or rather causing it and continually reviving it as the feuds killed it, was the one great source of unity—the Church in Scotland. All Scots were still of the one true Faith.*

*There are sincere men on all sides of all great controversies, but Henry VIII of England stands in history as an infamous, treacherous, and most cruel tyrant. Though victorious at Flodden, his taste of Scottish steel was so bitter that he preferred to conquer by fraud rather than by war. He saw a way to break the one great bond of national unity—the Church in Scotland. Constant civil war had left many Scottish lairds poor. The lands of the Church, left in comparative peace for centuries, were prosperous. Henry whispered in the ears of these impoverished nobles to enrich themselves by stealing from the House of God. Some took Henry's path to wealth. More would have done so, but they feared the anger of the young King of Scotland, James V. Though of that passionate nature which has often many sins to answer for, James had that strong faith in God and in eternal truths that makes a man repent and try to atone.*

## Virtue Discussion

1. Discuss this passage. Can you recall any incidents from the lives of the saints that demonstrate this virtue?
2. Consider a time in your life when you or someone you know practiced this virtue. What was the effect

of this action? Discuss at least two specific things you can do differently in your daily life to improve your practice of the virtue of peace. Do them!

# Chapter 12 – Last Stand of the Old Earl

## Vocabulary
1. *Shrovetide*: the few days preceding Ash Wednesday
2. *the sixth James*: King James VI of Scotland and King James I of England who reigned Scotland from 1567-1625 and England from 1603-1625
3. *scepter*: ruling power or authority; a staff held as a symbol of such authority
4. *the rack*: instrument of torture upon which a victim's body is stretched
5. *litter*: a stretcher for carrying sick or injured persons
6. *plaids*: rectangular woolen tartans (scarves) worn over the left shoulder by Scottish Highlanders
7. *Easter Communion*: the reception of Holy Communion (accompanied by the Sacrament of Penance and Reconciliation) as required by the Church each year between Ash Wednesday and Trinity Sunday
8. *surplice*: a long-sleeved tunic; a liturgical garment
9. *acolyte*: a person appointed to minister to the needs of the priest by assisting in the service at the altar and as needed in the celebration of the Holy Sacrifice of the Mass; an altar server
10. *dirk*: a short knife with a pointed blade; a dagger
11. *gilly*: a boy or young man; a young, male assistant
12. *curs*: mongrel dogs; cowardly persons
13. *guineas*: gold coins worth one pound, one shilling each

## Discussion Questions
1. What does the phrase, "a martyr in fact if not in name" mean? How can this idea also be applied to many of the saints?

2. The old Earl, as the godfather of the captain, implores him to reconsider his actions. Discuss the godparents' duties to their godchildren.
3. What do you think motivates Bertrand's actions? What is *your* primary motivation?

## Scripture References
1. "But the Master washed the feet of Judas and that same night was betrayed by him." Read Matthew 26:14-16 and 47-50, and John 13:1-30.
2. Regarding the Precious Blood of Jesus, read 1 Peter 1:17-21.

**Virtue – Fear of the Lord:** The gift of the Holy Spirit that fills us with awe and reverence for God; protects us from offending Him by sin

## Virtue Passage
Read the following passage to see how this virtue causes Captain Brent to change from an attacker to a defender of the Lord and his people:

*"Captain John Brent," said Sir Angus slowly, "I was your godfather in baptism. By the vows I took that day, I tell you that you have committed a grievous sin this day. The punishments of God Almighty are terrible."*

*"My orders, sir," growled the officer. "A soldier must obey orders."*

*"And since when do the orders of a king make it lawful to break the laws of the King of kings?"*

*There was a struggle on Brent's face. He was too good a man for such a trade.*

*"Come," he growled, "let's go. We have done enough of the devil's work for one day!"*

*The men seemed only too willing to obey. They had no wish to match swords with the great Sir Angus Gordon.*

*But Bertrand sprang forward.*

*"You white-livered cowards!" he roared. "Twenty seasoned veterans against one old fool and a fisherman's gilly! A thousand pounds' reward for the priest's body! The rubies on that chalice are worth rattlin' guineas! Here you stand like whipped curs in fear o' the lang-sword! Don't you know the old cutthroat has reached his doddering days?"*

*"If fight you will, fight I will!" shouted Brent. "But I draw for the other side! Perhaps God may forgive me the sins of this night!"*

*"He will forgive you," said Sir Angus.*

*The captain sprang forward, but paused and dropped on his knees as he passed the altar. He looked at the Blessed Sacrament, one sorrowful, pleading look. Then he took his place.*

## Virtue Discussion

1. Discuss this passage. Can you recall any incidents from the lives of the saints that demonstrate this virtue?
2. Consider a time in your life when you or someone you know practiced this virtue. What was the effect of this action? Discuss at least two specific things you can do differently in your daily life to improve your practice of the virtue of the fear of the Lord. Do them!

# Chapter 13 – Guardians of the King

## Vocabulary

1. *sacrilege*: a deliberate violation or desecration of sacred persons, objects or places; a sin against the virtue of religion
2. *paten*: a saucer-like dish of the same material as the chalice—gold-plated and consecrated by a bishop; holds the bread to be consecrated and later the Sacred Host
3. *corporal*: a square, white linen cloth upon which the chalice and paten are placed on the altar during Mass
4. *cuff*: an open-handed blow
5. *curry favor*: to seek to gain goodwill
6. *asunder*: into separate pieces; apart from each other
7. *babel*: a confusion of voices and other noises; from the Tower of Babel in Genesis 11:1-9
8. *buttery*: a small room for storing foods or wine; a pantry

## Discussion Questions

1. ". . .it is a sin to touch holy things." Discuss the sin of sacrilege (desecration). What might you have done if you were in the situation of the four children?
2. "The trustful prayer of a child is an arrow that pierces the Heart of God." Why are the prayers of children so powerful? (See Psalm 131.)
3. How are all Catholics called to be "Guardians of the King?"

## Scripture References

1. ". . .but the angel Gabriel could scarcely have been more welcome than Benson." Read the following

Biblical references to the angel Gabriel: Daniel 8:15-27, Daniel 9:20-27, and Luke 1:10-38.

2. Regarding "the light of the joy that shines on those who have suffered for the Lord our God," read Acts 6:8-15 in which the face of Stephen is described.

**Virtue – Prudence:** A moral (cardinal) virtue that helps us to discern the true good in every circumstance and to choose the right means of achieving it; sound judgment

## Virtue Passage

Read the following two paragraphs to see the virtue of prudence in action:

*Stephen looked with trembling reverence on the Sacred Host lying there so white and still. "O Lord" he prayed, "don't You see how it is? We don't know what we ought to do, and we must do something. We cannot leave You like this. Please forgive us if we make mistakes, and forgive us our sins so that we shall not be too bad to touch Your Sacred Body and most Precious Blood."*

*From that moment, both boys lost their fear and knew that the good Lord would reward with His eternal gratitude whatever poor, little, clumsy service they might render Him, now lying as if helpless, as if needing their care.*

## Virtue Discussion

1. Discuss this passage. Can you recall any incidents from the lives of the saints that illustrate prudence?
2. Consider a time in your life when you or someone you know practiced this virtue. What was the effect of this action? Discuss at least two specific things you can do differently in your daily life to improve your practice of the virtue of prudence. Do them!

# Chapter 14 – Glory of the Bitter End

## Vocabulary
1. *steward*: one who manages the household affairs of a large estate
2. *abominable*: thoroughly unpleasant and disagreeable; loathsome
3. *popish*: of or pertaining to the popes or the Roman Catholic Church; usually a derogatory term
4. *Our Lady in Harvest*: a feast day of the Blessed Virgin Mary celebrated on August 15—the Feast of the Assumption or Dormition
5. *retainer*: a servant or attendant who belongs to a family of high rank
6. *Scot of the Covenant*: a member of the National Church of Scotland, which opposed the Roman Catholic Church
7. *idolaters*: a derogatory term for Roman Catholics stemming from the mistaken idea that Catholics worship the Blessed Virgin Mary and the saints
8. *haycock*: a conical pile of hay left in the field to dry before storing
9. *Queen Bess*: daughter of King Henry VIII, Queen Elizabeth I of England reigned from 1533-1603
10. *standard*: a flag, banner or ensign of an army or country; the colors of a military unit
11. *Stephen*: a reference to St. Stephen, the first Christian martyr
12. *headsman*: an executioner who beheads condemned prisoners
13. *knave*: an unprincipled, deceitful servant

## Discussion Questions

1.  "A base nature cannot understand the kind of glory [the glory of dying for God] of which Sir Edward spoke." Analyze this statement.
2.  "No cause is dead while true hearts live" and ". . .the will of a mob is the will of the wind." How can you apply the wisdom of these quotations?

## Scripture References

1.  ". . .she be nigh the gates that be made o' pearl": Read of the New Jerusalem: Revelation 21:18-27.
2.  "Would I were worthy to fall under the banner of the King of kings, worthy of my place in the red-robed army led by Stephen." "Red-robed" usually refers to the clothing of martyrs. Read the story of the martyrdom of St. Stephen in Acts 7:51-60.

## Virtue – Love (Charity): A theological virtue (and fruit of the Holy Spirit) by which we love God above all things for His own sake, and our neighbor as ourselves for the love of God

## Virtue Passage

Read of Sir Angus' love of God in the following passage:

*"Sir Henry of Russell asks what I wish to say in answer to the charge of treason which now stains my knightly honor. There are stains that tell of shame, and there are stains that speak of glory. When they brought the standard back from Flodden Field, there was a stain upon it. Aye, a dark blot upon the fair silken banner from Dun Edin, but that stain was the lifeblood of a King. That torn and blood-stained banner is a sacred thing. Aye, a sacred thing. Now the Faith of the King who fell on Flodden Field is called treason against Scotland. This Faith is that*

47

*stain which lies on my honor as a Scottish knight. This stain is my glory as it was the glory of those that are no more. Would I were worthy to fall under the banner of the King of kings, worthy of my place in the red-robed army led by Stephen. Thank God for the honor done me, and stand for God and our Lady till we meet again.*

Read too of his love of neighbor as illustrated in this passage:

*"Allen," said the old Earl gently, "the sin of this lies on the judge, not upon the executioner. You will be merely doing your duty according to law. Do not bring trouble on yourself through love of me."*

*"It may be no sin in the eye of the law—queer laws they do be havin' these days! Was it your duty accordin' to law to send a cow to my brother's wife? They were no' your tenants more. If the widow and her wee bit bairns were starvin', what was that to you in the eye o' the law? But you sent the cow!"*

*"It is little I gave them, Allen. Do your work, lad. I shall bear you no ill will, nor will the good God lay this to your charge. Sir Henry is angry. He wilt make you suffer, my poor fellow."*

## Virtue Discussion

1. Discuss this passage. Can you recall any incidents from the lives of the saints that demonstrate charity?
2. Consider a time in your life when you or someone you know practiced this virtue. What was the effect of this action? Discuss at least two specific things you can do differently in your daily life to improve your practice of your love of neighbor. Do them!

# Chapter 15 – Splinter of the Lang-Sword

## Vocabulary
1. *salvos*: a sudden outburst of cheers or praise
2. *seraphim*: the highest rank of the nine choirs of angels; sit before God's throne, praising Him in their cries of "Holy, Holy, Holy" as in the *Sanctus* of the liturgy
3. *myriad*: large, infinite number; innumerable
4. *petulantly*: ill-temperedly; irritably

## Discussion Questions
1. Discuss the following quotation: "[Godfrey's] mind was too cunning to start a battle lost from the beginning." What did Godfrey perceive about Gordon?
2. How might you feel if you believed you were suffering and near death? What might happen when you realized that death was not soon, but the pain was to continue? What tactics might you use to stand firm in your faith?

## Scripture References
1. "His own battle horn was blowing." Read about the battle of Jericho in Joshua 6:1-20.
2. Gordon gained strength from the teaching of his mother (Deuteronomy 4:9), from those who had gone before him (Hebrews 13:7-8 and Psalm 78:5-7), from God's great love (Psalm 118:5-9), and from the sacred hearth-stone (1 Peter 2:4-7).

**Virtue – Fortitude:** A moral virtue that ensures firmness in difficulties and constancy in the pursuit of good; strengthens the resolve to resist temptations and enables one to overcome fear; courage; also a gift of the Holy Spirit

## Virtue Passage

This entire chapter resounds of fortitude. Re-read especially the following passage:

> The door creaked as it opened. Sir Roger was there with Godfrey at his elbow. The tutor drew in his breath with a hiss. Disappointment darkened Sir Roger's face. He had thought to find a lad worn weary with pain, petulantly defiant, but breaking. Gordon's hot words of a few hours ago had shown his self-control to be weakening. Here, strengthened from some unknown source, the boy stood before them. His face was swollen and twisted with pain, yet in his eyes there was no fear, no yielding, no weariness, but a look of joy deeper than the wrongs of earth, sweeter and stronger than human. Godfrey would have slipped out again. Though his soul was too grossly formed to comprehend the boy's exaltation, yet his mind was too cunning to start a battle lost from the beginning.

## Virtue Discussion

1. Discuss this passage. Can you recall any incidents from the lives of the saints that demonstrate fortitude?
2. Consider a time in your life when you or someone you know practiced this virtue. What was the effect of this action? Discuss at least two specific things you can do differently in your daily life to improve your practice of the virtue of fortitude. Do them!

# Chapter 16 – Escape

## Vocabulary
1. **Angelus**: a devotion to the Incarnation, commemorating the angel Gabriel's annunciation to the Blessed Virgin Mary; recited at six in the morning, noon, and six in the evening; the Angelus bells were rung nine times with a pause between every third ring for the space of one Our Father and one Hail Mary
2. *casement*: window that opens by means of hinges on one side
3. *must*: staleness; odor
4. *mote-filled*: full of specks; full of dust particles
5. *vial*: a small glass or plastic container used for storing liquids; the small neck can be plugged or capped

## Discussion Questions
1. "This was a day on earth to win heaven—not heaven come down to earth." Discuss the meaning of this statement.
2. What does Godfrey mean when he suggests, "Mend the folly with this [vial]"?

## Scripture References
1. Gordon hears the *Angelus* bells. Read about the Incarnation (which is what is celebrated in the *Angelus*) in Luke 1:26-38.
2. Gordon calls upon the Lord in his need. See Proverb 3:5, Mark 11:24, and Ephesians 6:10-18.

**Virtue – Temperance:** The moral virtue that moderates the attraction of pleasures and provides balance in the use of created goods; ensures the will's mastery over instincts and keeps desires within the limits of what is honorable

## Virtue Passage

This chapter provides an illustration of what can happen when decisions are not governed by temperance. Read the following passage to see how Godfrey and Uncle Roger have let their greed and pride determine their course of action—rather than the virtue of temperance:

"The foolish child will yield in the morning. You are always finding fault."

"My Lord, Gordon has a brain; he will not be twice fooled by any man. Yet there is one way. . ."

"And that?"

"Tomorrow we shall go to him—you and I—tell him his courage has won our hearts, we must respect a Faith that can make so young a lad so great a hero, give him full liberty to practice his religion—privately—"

"Of all the follies? Are you mad?"

"Mend the folly, my good Sir Roger, mend the folly with this."

The tutor held up a vial that gleamed red in the candlelight.

"You mean—"

"Oh, its action is very gentle, my Lord. As the warm days come—a paleness, a weakness, just a slight malaria; yet in the autumn all the gentlefolk of the countryside will come to the funeral of this promising boy, and the mourning uncle—well, it will all be very sad—but, of course, the mourning uncle will be Earl of Ravenhurst."

## Virtue Discussion

1. Discuss this passage. Can you recall any incidents from the lives of the saints that demonstrate temperance?

2. Consider a time in your life when you or someone you know practiced this virtue. What was the effect of this action? Discuss at least two specific things you can do differently in your daily life to improve your practice of the virtue of temperance. Do them!

# Chapter 17 – Secret Passages

## Vocabulary
*Muckle*: much; a large amount or number

## Discussion Questions
1. "Ah, how sweet is God's own air!" How often we forget to thank God for His many simple gifts. What gifts can you begin to thank God for each day?
2. Imagine being in the dark—lost, tired, and scared—and being grabbed by something or someone. How might you react? Speculate on who may have grabbed Gordon.

## Scripture References
1. Regarding escape, read Psalm 124, Proverb 11:8, and Acts 9:23-25.
2. "I have been praying for a drop of water. Now the good Lord has given me a drop into it, instead of a drop of it." Water is a gift from God. Read Isaiah 58:11, John 4:10-14, John 7:37-38, and Revelation 21:6.

**Virtue – Knowledge:** A gift of the Holy Spirit that enables us to see God reflected in all creation but to see all created things as nothing in themselves so we might desire God alone; perfects our faith; allows us to put creatures to their right use and to see God's care in all that happens to us

## Virtue Passage
Gordon's faith allows him to see God in all creation. Find his exclamations of "God's own air" and "God's good out-of-doors" in this chapter.

## Virtue Discussion

1. Discuss this passage. Can you recall any incidents from the lives of the saints that demonstrate this virtue?

2. Consider a time in your life when you or someone you know practiced this virtue. What was the effect of this action? Discuss at least two specific things you can do differently in your daily life to improve your practice of the virtue of knowledge. Do them!

# Chapter 18 – Sir James of Gordon

## Vocabulary
1. *coronet*: a small crown worn by princes, princesses, and other nobles
2. *escutcheon*: a shield or shield-shaped emblem upon which the coat of arms is displayed
3. *riven*: torn apart; split into pieces
4. *cistern*: a receptacle for holding water; a tank for catching rainwater

## Discussion Questions
1. What does Sir James' statement, "No brass in the ringing of that coin, boy!" imply?
2. "Now, sweet Mother, you bring him to me." "The Blessed Mother of God has watched over you." Discuss what it means to entrust someone or something to our Lord's mother. Consider consecrating yourself and your family to the Blessed Virgin Mary.

## Scripture References
1. Gordon's father rejoiced when he heard that Gordon was true to the Faith. Read and discuss 2 Samuel 22:26-27, Psalm 89:2, and Colossians 1:21-23 on faithfulness.
2. Read about courage in Psalm 44:19-20 and about weariness in Isaiah 40:29-31.

## Virtue – Generosity (Long-suffering or Longanimity):
A fruit of the Holy Spirit; teaches us to consider the future good and to wait over an extended time with patience and constancy; includes restraint in demanding justice

## Virtue Passage
Find examples of this virtue in the words and actions of Sir James within this chapter.

## Virtue Discussion
1. Discuss this passage. Can you recall any incidents from the lives of the saints that demonstrate long-suffering?
2. Consider a time in your life when you or someone you know practiced this virtue. What was the effect of this action? Discuss at least two specific things you can do differently in your daily life to improve your practice of the virtue of generosity. Do them!

# Chapter 19 – Muckle John

## Vocabulary
1. *heather*: low evergreen shrub; grown in the northern hemisphere in dense masses; scale-like leaves and small purplish-pink flowers
2. *rude*: vigorous; sturdy
3. *doublet*: a close-fitting jacket
4. *boudoir*: a woman's bedroom
5. *dirk*: stab with a knife
6. *sentinel's*: belonging to someone employed to keep watch; a lookout man's
7. *hackbut*: firearm with a long barrel; a matchlock gun

## Discussion Questions
1. Muckle John is gentleness itself in his care for Gordon, "yet in his eyes was the coming fury." What might this mean? What vow does he make to Clan Gordon to avenge Gordon's injuries?
2. What plan does Godfrey contrive when confronted with members of Clan Gordon?

## Scripture References
1. Muckle John says, "Keep the name o' God off that foul tongue o' yers!" Read about God's name in these Scripture passages: Exodus 3:13-15, Psalm 113: 1-3, Isaiah 9:5, Jeremiah 10:6, and Philippians 2:5-11.
2. Persecuted for his faith, Gordon suffers injury and illness. Read about St. Paul, who also suffered for his faith: Acts 14:19-22, Acts 16:16-24, and Acts 21:27-32. What are you willing to suffer for the Faith?

**Virtue – Gentleness (Mildness):** Tenderness in disposition and behavior; a fruit of the Holy Spirit that perfects love and tempers justice by avoiding unnecessary action

## Virtue Passage

Re-read Muckle John's gentleness with Gordon in the following passage. Despite his gruff exterior, notice how Muckle John displays this virtue again later in the story.

> Muckle John sat by the lad all day. Now and then, he sponged the hot body gently, so gently that the boy did not stir, or he roused the lad to give him a drink of soup. Hour after hour, he watched for a glimmer of returning consciousness. And all the while, the beads slipped through his iron-muscled fingers as he pleaded with God's Mother for his chieftain and for Clan Gordon.

## Virtue Discussion

1. Discuss this passage. Can you recall any incidents from the lives of the saints that demonstrate gentleness?
2. Consider a time in your life when you or someone you know practiced this virtue. What was the effect of this action? Discuss at least two specific things you can do differently in your daily life to improve your practice of the virtue of gentleness. Do them!

# Chapter 20 – Gordon for God and Our Lady

## Vocabulary
1. *lung fever*: infection of the lungs; pneumonia
2. *laggers*: stragglers; those who hang back or proceed with extreme slowness
3. *lief*: willingly; readily
4. *Ald Black Hornie*: the devil
5. *extremity*: grave necessity or distress
6. *scullions*: kitchen servants; those employed to do menial tasks and hard labor
7. *Baltimore*: possibly George Calvert, First Baron Baltimore (1580-1632) and founder in spirit of the colony of Maryland
8. *heath*: small evergreen shrubs; heather
9. *kirkyard*: a churchyard; a cemetery situated next to a church
10. *Davy's locker*: Davy Jones' locker; a fictional place at the bottom of the sea; a resting place for those who die at sea
11. *brigs*: two-masted sailing ships
12. *kith an' kin*: friends and relatives

## Discussion Questions
1. Many have "gone down with the evil tide." Strong Christian friends and frequent reception of the sacraments are important aids in remaining true to the faith. How can you apply these ideas into your own life?
2. "Without priests and sacraments, the Faith must die among our children." Consider what you can do to increase vocations in our country.
3. "Never to know Scotland more; never to smell the wind o' mornin' blowin' fresh fra' o'er the heath. . . ."

How hard would it be for you to move to a strange country in order to safely practice your faith?

## Scripture References

1. Read Proverbs 13:20 and 22:24-25, Ecclesiastes 4:9-10, and Sirach 6:14-17 on Christian companionship.
2. Regarding revenge and vengeance, read Leviticus 19:17-18, Sirach 28:1-11, and Romans 12:17-21.

**Virtue – Wisdom:** A gift of the Holy Spirit that enables us to know the purpose and plan of God; allows us to see things as God sees them and to penetrate the truths of our faith

## Virtue Passage

Read the plan proposed by Sir James to see wisdom in action:

> "I have a better plan to offer. Erecting a fortress means the beginning of a feud and the end of that we all know. More Gordons would die in battle. More orphans wail for bread. The cause for which our fathers stood is dead in Scotland, though not forever. It is to the New World we should turn our eyes. There the old cause lives anew."
>
> "Aye!" shouted the captain of the guard, "aye, my Lord, would ye lead us there? That is a plan worth hearing if sailors' tales be true: red men roaming the wildwood and trading you furs fit for a king's robe to the tune of a few glass beads—aye, lads, and Spanish gold!"
>
> "No, no! I am not promising fortune in the New World. It is not a land where gold is picked up by the handful and jewels shine like drops of dew on a May morning. These are but sailors' tales. Those who follow me to Maryland must go for one reason: to

find a spot where we can be free to worship the Lord our God.

"There are few priests now in Scotland. Soon even these will be gone. Without priests and sacraments, the Faith must die among our children.

"Years ago, Baltimore told me much about his colony. Do not hope for gold, for you will find hardships instead. On the way, we shall suffer. We may face starvation. In Maryland we shall suffer much, at least during the months before the first harvest. Even after the worst is over, there will be hard work and grinding poverty all our lives.

"But we shall be free men in a free land. We shall adore God as our souls cry out to do. We shall rear our children in the Faith."

## Virtue Discussion

1. Discuss this passage. Can you recall any incidents from the lives of the saints that demonstrate wisdom?

2. Consider a time in your life when you or someone you know practiced this virtue. What was the effect of this action? Discuss at least two specific things you can do differently in your daily life to improve your practice of the virtue of wisdom. Do them!

# Chapter 21 – Rock Raven No More

## Vocabulary
1. *barque*: a sailing ship with three masts
2. *Extreme Unction*: For centuries, the term used for the Sacrament of Anointing of the Sick; extreme as it was used when death seemed likely and unction as the person is anointed with oil; when death seems imminent, the Sacraments of Penance and Reconciliation, and Holy Eucharist (Viaticum) may also be given
3. *rills*: small brooks
4. *corporal*: a white linen cloth on which the Host and chalice are placed during the celebration of the Eucharist

## Discussion Questions
1. For what does Margaret ask forgiveness?
2. Before receiving the sacrament of Holy Eucharist, Gordon desires confession—even though he had participated in this sacrament only days prior. Are you as conscientious about the state of your soul before receiving the Holy Eucharist? Always remember Who it is that you are welcoming into your heart.
3. What is the "Bread of the strong?" Why is it referred to in this way?

## Scripture References
1. "And he was alone when he suffered." Read Mark 15:34 and Philippians 2:26-27.
2. "Then Stephen anointed the boy." Read about anointing, which confers a special blessing: 1 Samuel 16:13, Luke 4:16-21, John 12:3, and James 5:14-15.

**Virtue – Charity:** The theological virtue (and a fruit of the Holy Spirit) by which we love God above all things for His own sake, and our neighbor as ourselves for the love of God

## Virtue Passage

Consider the charity exhibited in the life of Fr. Stephen. Re-read his actions in this chapter:

A shadow darkened the doorway. Jean tiptoed in, lit the candles, and knelt. Father Stephen entered and laid his Sacred Burden on the linen cloth.

"Gordon," he said in his clear, low voice, "I am going to give you Extreme Unction."

The eyes brightened, then grew puzzled. "Confession first—"

"If there is anything to confess. You have nothing to tell, have you?"

"Can't remember . . . maybe I haven't had time . . . to be bad."

"Blessed are the days when we have no time to be bad! So, do not worry. Say in your heart, 'My Jesus, I love Thee. Forgive me.'" Then Stephen anointed the boy. Not much of evil had he ever known. Not far had his feet gone astray. And then, Gordon's eyes rested on the Sacred Host. Nothing else he seemed to see.

"Aye," murmured Muckle John, "an' tell Him yer father an' mother an' all o' the clan ha' need o' our lad. Mayhap He'll leave ye bide wi' us, for sure the good Lord be kind."

The eyes closed. Margaret's head sank on the couch, her hand clenched on the cross. But Stephen whispered softly, "Sleeping, only sleeping with the good Lord in his breast."

\* \* \* \* \*

The day fled swiftly. Inside the cottage, the ebb and flow of the rosary still beat on the eternal shore, but the song in those waves was of hope. Outside, the silent folk sped on errands to and from the boats or went on noiseless feet through Ald Donald's door to pour into Stephen's patient ear their sorrows and their sins and to come out again with hope-lit eyes and firm-set lips.

A little after midnight, the altar was prepared. The Holy Sacrifice was offered, solemnly, silently, lest some sacrilegious band steal upon them through the darkness, and to each was given the Bread of the strong.

The sentinel on the seaward tower of Castle Ravenhurst watched the fishers putting out to sea in the dawn. "Fair day coming," was all he thought.

He did not see the tall, gaunt figure in a long gray cloak standing on a cliff and holding out his crucifix in blessing until the ships rounded a headland and could see Rock Raven no more.

Then Stephen Douglas turned and strode back into the forest to wander, hound-tracked, starving, and alone, happy if he found a soul who even in the last dread hour would make its peace with God.

No man knew when the good Lord called him home.

But one year when the snows of Ben Ender were slipping away in merry, tinkling rills over the stones and under the mosses, Edwin found him. His face was strangely beautiful, lying there host-white on a corporal of virgin snow.

## Virtue Discussion

1. Discuss this passage. Can you recall any incidents from the lives of the saints that demonstrate this virtue?
2. Consider a time in your life when you or someone you know practiced this virtue. What was the effect of this action? Discuss at least two specific things you can do differently in your daily life to improve your practice of charity. Do them!

# Chapter 22 – In the Hollow of God's Hand

## Vocabulary

1. *calking*: the waterproof filler applied to make a watertight seal
2. *lugger*: a small fishing boat with two or three masts and several jib sails
3. *derelict*: that which has been abandoned
4. *spar*: a wooden or metal pole used to support rigging and sails
5. *prate*: idle talk; rapid speech; chatter
6. *larboard*: port; the left side of the ship facing forward
7. *growler*: a large mass of ice floating at sea
8. *jetty*: a structure that sticks out into a body of water to influence the tides or protect the shoreline; a pier or wharf
9. *tother*: the other
10. *amidships*: near or towards the middle of the ship; between the stern and bow of the vessel
11. *plying*: working steadily

## Discussion Questions

1. Discuss the following quotation: "Pray more an' prate less." What does this mean? How can you apply the wisdom of this saying? How can you charitably help others apply this axiom to their lives as well?
2. What does it mean to be "more noble by nature than by blood?"

## Scripture References

1. Read Exodus 33:22 and Isaiah 49:15-16.
2. Read Luke 19:1-10 about someone else who climbed a tree to see something or some One.

**Virtue – Counsel:** The gift of the Holy Spirit that allows God's light to guide us in practical matters, enabling us to judge promptly and rightly, especially in difficult situations

## Virtue Passage

Browse through this chapter paying special attention to the decisions made by Muckle John and Sir James. Find several passages that highlight this virtue and how it is practiced in the daily life of both these characters.

## Virtue Discussion

1. Discuss this passage. Can you recall any incidents from the lives of the saints that demonstrate this virtue?
2. Consider a time in your life when you or someone you know practiced the virtue of counsel. What was the effect of this action? Discuss at least two specific things you can do differently in your daily life to improve your practice of this virtue. Do them!

# Chapter 23 – Our Lady's Home

## Vocabulary
1. *temples*: that part of the face in front of the ears and above the check bones; the sides of the forehead
2. *cove*: a small sheltered bay or inlet on the shoreline
3. *slash*: an open area of land in a forest that is littered with debris from clearing
4. *fodder*: feed for livestock; coarsely chopped hay or straw; the stalks and leaves of any cereal plant
5. *fallow*: land left unplanted during a growing season; may be plowed
6. *bays*: reddish-brown horses, usually with black manes and tails

## Discussion Questions
1. "Second rosary. . .for the eternal well-being and safe return of our George."Remember that each prayer we say—each sacrifice we make—merits grace. Begin to offer this grace for a certain intention, just as the Abell family did in their rosary.
2. "Many times Daddy said, 'Thanks be to God and to His holy Mother!'" Discuss how you and your family can help each other acquire the powerful holy habit of thanking God aloud.

## Scripture References
1. Read John 17:9-21, Ephesians 1:15-17, 1 Thessalonians 1:2, and 2 Timothy 1:3 on remembering others in prayer.
2. Read Psalms 118:1, 118:28-29, 136:1-3, and 138; Philippians 4:6 and 1 Thessalonians 5:18 on giving thanks.

**Virtue – Joy:** The feeling aroused by the expectation or possession of a desired good; a fruit of the Holy Spirit; originates in the will while pleasure originates in the senses

## Virtue Passage

Imagine Gordon's joy in the knowledge that help has arrived for the shipwrecked clan members. Consider the joy of Clan Gordon as they establish themselves safely in Mary's Land to practice their faith without persecution.

## Virtue Discussion

1. Discuss this passage. Can you recall any incidents from the lives of the saints that demonstrate true joy?
2. Consider a time in your life when you or someone you know practiced this virtue. What was the effect of this action? Discuss at least two specific things you can do differently in your daily life to improve your practice of the virtue of joy. Do them!

# Epilogue

## Vocabulary
1. *while Puritan soldiers glared*: The successor of King James VI of Scotland (King James I of England) was Charles I who reigned from 1625 until his execution in 1649. Throughout his reign, Charles I fought with Parliament as well as the Puritans
2. *Cromwell*: Oliver Cromwell (1599-1658), controversial Lord Protector of England, Ireland and Scotland from 1653-1658

## Discussion Questions
1. ". . .jottings of God's finger on the shifting dunes of time." Discuss the meaning of this phrase.
2. Edwin suggests that Roger had a conversion in "the last dread hour." Review Roger's attitude toward Jesus' Precious Blood in this chapter. Discuss how easy it is to come under the influence of power, prestige, and money—especially when friends reinforce those attitudes. What can you do to avoid this pitfall and keep focused on eternity?

## Scripture References
1. Read and discuss the following Biblical passages that relate to time: Job 16:22, Psalm 39:5-7, Psalm 90:4, Ecclesiastes 1:4, James 4:13-15, and 2 Peter 3:8-9.
2. Read about worldliness: Matthew 24:36-44, Luke 16:13, Romans 8:5-9, Romans 12:2, and Titus 2:11-13.

**Virtue – Hope:** Virtue by which we desire the Kingdom of Heaven and eternal life as our happiness, placing our trust in Christ's promises and relying not on our own strength but the grace of the Holy Spirit; a gift of the Holy Spirit

## Virtue Passage
Re-read the Epilogue, remembering that God loves all His children. We must always trust in Him and His greatest attribute of mercy.

## Virtue Discussion
1. Discuss this passage. Can you recall any incidents from the lives of the saints that demonstrate hope?
2. Consider a time in your life when you or someone you know practiced this virtue. What was the effect of this action? Discuss at least two specific things you can do differently in your daily life to improve your practice of the virtue of hope. Do them!

# Works of Mercy and the Beatitudes

While the virtues and the gifts and fruits of the Holy Spirit help us to understand what type of personality traits Jesus wants us to develop, the corporal and spiritual works of mercy, and the Beatitudes help us to put our faith into action. The works of mercy are "charitable actions by which we come to the aid of our neighbor in his spiritual and bodily necessities" (*Catechism of the Catholic Church* ¶2447)—good deeds done for others. According to the *Compendium* of the *Catechism of the Catholic Church*, the Beatitudes "depict the very countenance of Jesus" and "characterize authentic Christian life" (¶360). They are the perfection of the Christian life.

Below are three matching exercises, one each for the spiritual works of mercy, the corporal works of mercy, and the Beatitudes. Scan the chapter from *Outlaws of Ravenhurst* listed on the left. Find an action from that chapter that corresponds with the appropriate work of mercy or Beatitude on the right. Possible answers are provided on pages 76-78, but keep in mind that other answers are defensible. From your memory of the book, discuss other works of mercy and Beatitudes exhibited by the characters.

Additional (blank) charts are included so that readers may begin to track the practice of the Beatitudes and works of mercy in their daily lives.

(As the *Catechism of the Catholic Church* speaks only generally of the works of mercy, the fourteen works of mercy listed below are the Church's traditional works of mercy as provided in *The Baltimore Catechism* of 1891. The Beatitudes are from Matthew 5:3-11 in the *New American* translation.)

## Corporal Works of Mercy in *Outlaws*

| | |
|---|---|
| Chapter 18 | Visit the imprisoned |
| Chapter 20 | Bury the dead |
| Chapter 14 | Feed the hungry |
| Chapter 3 | Shelter the homeless |
| Chapter 21 | Visit the sick |
| Chapter 1 | Give drink to the thirsty |
| Chapter 18 | Clothe the naked |

## Spiritual Works of Mercy in *Outlaws*

| | |
|---|---|
| Chapter 8 | Counsel the doubtful |
| Chapter 3 | Pray for the living and the dead |
| Chapter 21 | Comfort the sorrowful |
| Chapter 20 | Admonish the sinner |
| Chapter 7 | Instruct the ignorant |
| Chapter 18 | Bear wrongs patiently |
| Chapter 20 | Forgive all injuries |

## Beatitudes in *Outlaws*

| Chapter 13 | Blessed are the clean of heart |
| --- | --- |
| Chapter 22 | Blessed are the poor in spirit |
| Chapter 14 | Blessed are the merciful |
| Chapter 14 | Blessed are they who hunger and thirst for righteousness |
| Chapter 20 | Blessed are the peacemakers |
| Chapter 6 | Blessed are they who mourn (over injustice) |
| Chapter 3 | Blessed are the meek |

**Optional exercise:** Choose a character and write an essay using incidents from the book to illustrate how this character models the virtues, gifts and fruits of the Holy Spirit, works of mercy, and Beatitudes. Use direct quotations of their conversations and cite specific actions to strengthen your character analysis. You may also choose a character who is weak in these Christ-like characteristics. In your essay, discuss how different his/her life would be if he/she practiced these virtues.

# Answer Key for Matching Exercises
## Corporal Works of Mercy Answer Key

| | |
|---|---|
| "You are in a cell of this castle!" "That I am." | Visit the imprisoned |
| "All the clan be goin', save Edwin. His ald mother be past ninety and bedridden. He can no come till he lays her in the kirkyard." | Bury the dead |
| *If the widow and her wee bit bairns were starvin', what was that to you in the eye o' the law? But you sent the cow!"* | Feed the hungry |
| "Father Cornwall found you sitting by the roadside and brought you to us. I set you on Mary's knee beside Joel, and so far as love and care go, you have been ours ever since." | Shelter the homeless |
| Father Stephen entered and laid his Sacred Burden on the linen cloth. | Visit the sick |
| "Hush!" came the man's low command in a tone that would have been menacing except that it was so deeply kind. "Drink." He drew a flask from his cloak. | Give drink to the thirsty |
| "Hald him easy whiles I wrap him up in my plaid". . ."Clad in rags, muddy, stiff wi' cold. . ." | Clothe the naked |

These are only a few illustrations of the corporal works of mercy in action. Challenge yourself to find others in the story.

## Spiritual Works of Mercy Answer Key

| | |
|---|---|
| "Never allow anyone to come between you and your mother, or between you and your God. These two friends are true." | Counsel the doubtful |
| "We'll say the beads every day till we know that you are safe." | Pray for the living and the dead |
| "No, no! We can hope! We must hope still!" | Comfort the sorrowful |
| "Vengeance is sin, Muckle John. . .Because Roger has wounded the heart of Christ by sin, need you sin also?" | Admonish the sinner |
| "Oh, no, Godfrey! Are the oaks dead because the leaves have fallen? Neither is the Church of God dead!" | Instruct the ignorant |
| "When a man faces life imprisonment in a doorless pit thirty feet below the land where God's sun is shining, he has the choice of three things. . ." | Bear wrongs patiently |
| "Do not judge poor Roger overhard. . .Poor fellow, he has gone down with the evil tide." | Forgive all injuries |

These are only a few illustrations of the spiritual works of mercy in action. Challenge yourself to find others in the story.

Janet P. McKenzie

## The Beatitudes Answer Key

| | |
|---|---|
| *The trustful prayer of a child is an arrow that pierces the Heart of God.* | Blessed are the clean of heart |
| ". . .No lives were lost. Only our treasured goods and our chest of gold are gone. God's Mother will provide." | Blessed are the poor in spirit |
| *". . .the sin of this lies on the judge, not upon the execution-er. You will be merely doing your duty according to law."* | Blessed are the merciful |
| *"When I am Earl, I shall take up the battle where my grandfather lays it down!"* | Blessed are they who hunger and thirst for righteousness |
| "Erecting a fortress means the beginning of a feud and the end of that we all know." | Blessed are the peacemakers |
| Margaret was not weeping; she had borne her pain too long for that. | Blessed are they who mourn |
| "Do as you are bid." "Yes, Mother." | Blessed are the meek |

## My Practice of the Corporal Works of Mercy

| Action and Date | Work of Mercy |
|---|---|
|  | Visit the imprisoned |
|  | Bury the dead |
|  | Feed the hungry |
|  | Shelter the homeless |
|  | Visit the sick |
|  | Give drink to the thirsty |
|  | Clothe the nakes |

## My Practice of the Spiritual Works of Mercy

| Action and Date | Work of Mercy |
|---|---|
| | Counsel the doubtful |
| | Pray for the living and the dead |
| | Comfort the sorrowful |
| | Admonish the sinner |
| | Instruct the ignorant |
| | Bear wrongs patiently |
| | Forgive all injuries |

# My Practice of the Beatitudes

| Action and Date | Beatitude |
| --- | --- |
| | Blessed are the clean of heart |
| | Blessed are the poor in spirit |
| | Blessed are the merciful |
| | Blessed are they who hunger and thirst for righteous |
| | Blessed are the peacemakers |
| | Blessed are they who mourn (for injustice) |
| | Blessed are the meek |
| | Blessed are the merciful |

# More RACE for Heaven Products

**RACE for Heaven study guides** use Mary Fabyan Windeatt's saint biographies to teach the Catholic faith to all members of your family. Written with your family's various learning levels in mind, these flexible study guides succeed as stand-alone unit studies or supplements to your regular curriculum. Thirty to sixty minutes per day will allow your family to experience:

☑ The spirituality and holy habits of the saints
☑ Lively family discussions on important faith topics
☑ Increased critical thinking and reading comprehension skills
☑ Quality read-aloud time with Catholic "living books"
☑ Enhanced knowledge of Catholic doctrine and the Bible
☑ History and geography incorporated into saintly literature
☑ Writing projects based on secular and Catholic historical events and characters

Purchase these guides individually or in the following grade-level packages (Grades are determined solely on the length of each book in the series.):

**Grades 3-4:** *St. Thomas Aquinas, The Story of the "Dumb Ox"; St. Catherine of Siena, The Girl Who Saw Saints in the Sky; Patron Saint of First Communicants, The Story of Blessed Imelda Lambertini;* and *The Miraculous Medal, The Story of Our Lady's Appearances to St. Catherine Labouré*

**Grade 5:** *St. Rose, First Canonized Saint of the Americas; St. Martin de Porres, The Story of the Little Doctor* *of Lima, Peru; King David and His Songs, A Story of the Psalms;* and *Blessed Marie of New France, The Story of the First Missionary Sisters in Canada*

**Grade 6:** *St. Dominic, Preacher of the Rosary and Founder of the Dominicans; St. Benedict, The Story of the Father of the Western Monks; The Children of Fatima and Our Lady's Message to the World;* and *St. John Masias, Marvelous Dominican Gatekeeper of Lima, Peru*

**Grade 7:** *The Little Flower, The Story of St. Therese of the Child Jesus; St. Hyacinth, The Story of the Apostle of the North; Curé of Ars, The Story of St. John Vianney, Patron Saint of Parish Priests;* and *St. Louis de Montfort, The Story of Our Lady's Slave*

**Grade 8:** *Pauline Jaricot, Foundress of the Living Rosary and the Society for the Propagation of Faith; St. Francis Solano, Wonder-Worker of the New World and Apostle of Argentina & Peru; St. Paul the Apostle, The Story of the Apostle to the Gentiles;* and *St. Margaret Mary, Apostle of the Sacred Heart*

***The Windeatt Dictionary: Pre-Vatican II Terms and Catholic Words from Mary Fabyan Windeatt's Saint Biographies*** explains over 450 Catholic terms and expressions used in this popular saint biography series. Indispensable in expanding knowledge and practice of the Catholic faith, this book provides a ready access for the Catholic vocabulary words used in the RACE for Heaven Windeatt study guides. This dictionary also includes a Catholic book report resource that contains suggestions for forty-five Catholic book reports: fourteen writing projects, ten book report activities, and twenty-one topics for saint biographies.

*Graced Encounters with Mary Fabyan Windeatt's Saints: 344 Ways to Imitate the Holy Habits of the Saints* is a compilation of the "Growing in Holiness" sections of RACE for Heaven's Catholic study guides for the Windeatt saint biography series and presents 344 examples of saintly behavior, one for nearly every chapter in each of these twenty biographies. Enhance your encounter with the saints by practicing the models of devotion, service, penance, prayer, and virtue offered in this guide.

*Communion with the Saints: A Family Preparation Program for First Communion and Beyond in the Spirit of St. Therese* imitates St. Therese of the Child Jesus and her family who studied and prayed for sixty-nine days in anticipation of Therese's First Holy Communion. Modeling this preparation, the *Communion with the Saints* program will help any family find renewed fervor in the reception of the Eucharist. This resource includes a chapter-by-chapter study of the following four books:

- *The Little Flower, The Story of Saint Therese of the Child Jesus*—to provide the foundation of God's love for us and to encourage a desire for holiness
- *The Children of Fatima and Our Lady's Message to the World*—to show the sinfulness of our world and the need to avoid sin
- *The Patron Saint of First Communicants, The Story of Blessed Imelda Lambertini*—to inspire devotion to the Sacrament of Holy Communion
- *The King of the Golden City* by Mother Mary Loyola—to illustrate Jesus' Presence as a source of grace necessary to live a holy life

Each of the sixty-nine days of preparation includes read-aloud selections with enrichment activities, meditational readings, catechism lessons, and plenty of practical application to promote a growth in holiness and sanctity. Weekend suggestions include a list of over thirty-five family projects. The use of *My First Communion Journal* is encouraged with this program.

*My First Communion Journal in Imitation of Saint Therese of the Child Jesus* provides a lasting keepsake of a child's First Holy Communion. Saint Therese of the Child Jesus and her family studied and prayed for sixty-nine days prior to Therese's First Holy Communion. This journal imitates that family model of preparation for the reception of the Most Holy Eucharist. Each daily entry contains a stanza of a poem composed by Saint Therese, a quotation from Saint Faustina Kowalska's diary *(Divine Mercy in My Soul)*, or a Scripture quotation. Two weekly themes—a floral theme in imitation of Saint Therese and a battle theme molded from the teachings of Saint Paul—are offered with accompanying weekly passages from Scripture suitable for memorization. This journal may be completed in conjunction with the *Communion with the Saints* program or used separately.

*The King of the Golden City Study Edition* is a new edition of a book that was originally published in 1921. This treasure of a book was written in response to a student's appeal for instructions along with "little stories" to help her prepare for Holy Communion. To fulfill this request, Mother Loyola of the Bar Convent in York, England, wrote a simple story that illustrates Jesus' desire to share an intimate relationship with each one of His children. This new edition contains some updated language, but quite deliberately, does not contain any pictures. Readers, as they progress through this story, will form a mental image of their King, one as unique and personal as their own relationship with Him. The study sections assist with the allegory, connect to the Bible as well as to the catechism, and explore the art of prayer in the spirit of the three Carmelite Doctors of the Church. Although written over eighty-five years ago for a young child, this book remains a timeless masterpiece of Catholic literature suitable for all ages.

*Reading the Saints: Lists of Catholic Books for Children Plus Book Collecting Tips for the Home and School Library* (formerly entitled *Saintly Resources*) is a valuable tool for Catholic home educators, classroom teachers, and collectors of Catholic juvenile books. *Reading the Saints* will help you discover living books from such popular out-of-print Catholic juvenile series as Catholic Treasury, Vision Books, and American Background Books as well as current series books for young Catholics. Use this book to find:

- Over 800 Catholic books listed by author, series, reading level, century, and geographical location
- More than 275 authors of saint biographies, historical fiction, and poetry written for Catholic juvenile readers
- Publishers of Catholic children's books, present and past
- Helpful advice for collecting and caring for used books
- Hundreds of age-appropriate, accessible living books to enrich your study of the Catholic Church's

rich heritage of saints and notable Catholic historical figures
- Information on how to build and maintain your own library of Catholic juvenile books
- Inspiring quotations about book collecting, reading, and the love of books

*Alternative Book Reports for Catholic Students* contains forty-five book report ideas that encourage critical thinking for ages seven to fourteen. These ideas are intended to provoke a reflection on those themes and topics that support and encourage Catholic living as well as some that may conflict with our Faith. Many report topics require an examination of our personal faith life and prompt us to take a lesson from the book to strengthen our own faith in God. Activities vary from written exercises to creative art projects and include twenty-one topics specifically designed for saint biographies. Other activities can be used within a group or family.

**To Order:** You may email race4hvn@hughes.net or order at RACEforHeaven.com. MasterCard, Discover, VISA, American Express, Paypal, checks, and money orders accepted.

www.ingramcontent.com/pod-product-compliance
Lightning Source LLC
Chambersburg PA
CBHW060953040426

42445CB00011B/1136